More Feathers for

My Wings

Medal of Distinction

John Underhill

ISBN: 978-1-954850-73-6

Dedication

This book is dedicated to my wife and my daughter for always being there at my side for support. I am proud to stand for all the officers that went beyond the line of duty and cared for people's lives.

Acknowledgment

Thank you to all the people I've met in my travels over the years—some of you I kept in touch with, some of you I have not, but still have memories of good and bad times. To my retired Chief Jack Stratton, thank you. To my good friends, John Cupa and Max Strausbaugh, thank you. Also, thanks to my brothers, Joe and Jack, who are both retired and caring people. Thank you to Maureen Reintjes, Director of Search KC and Missouri Missing. Last, the publishing company that put up with me and helped me put this together.

CONTENTS

About the Author

John Underhill is an author who lives in Kansas City, Missouri, with his wife. The two have a child named Ian. John was born in Alhambra, California and grew up, most of his life, in California before moving to Kansas City, Missouri and where he bought a ranch house. *This book will show that all the things you do in your career will affect your life and your health and it's not all "rosy". The badge will always be a symbol of trust, faith, and integrity.*

Glad to still be alive and see the sunrise.

Preface

This book was written to show a person can have 9 lives, and the things people in Law Enforcement can see every day. We are human and we have feelings just like anyone else. I received the medal of distinction for a lot of these incidents listed in this book, I was unable to put it all in this book. I also received the valor award by the VFW organization; my best job was being a Police Detective. After I retired, I was a Private Investigator and have over 7000 pro bono hours on Missing Person cases.

These are some of my stats:

- *40 suspects arrested in a three-month period that were armed*

- *22 stolen vehicles occupied in a three-month period*

- *3 hundred thousand dollars in stolen property/ Traffic stop of two U-Hauls in one month from residential burglaries*

- *30 search warrants in one month for narcotics*

- *One of the highest Heroin seizures in the county!*

Chapter 1
Only the Beginning

As a result of my ancestors having achieved affluence, my early childhood was relatively normal. Growing up with three pesky brothers, me being the youngest, could be described as a little wayward, but I was a good kid. I lived with my siblings, a doting mother, and a distant father. My mother and father had a nurturing demeanor. They were always there for us and helped us out whenever we needed their assistance. My father was the kind of man who compulsively worked hard and long hours.

He left us under the care and protection of our mother. My mother was a kind-hearted and compassionate woman; she was driven purely by her innate altruistic reasons to help us as much as she could. She would put everything aside and drive me to the police station after school or on weekends. Additionally, she would frequently offer money to me without letting my father know. I was always the kind of kid who was good-natured; I had an amiable personality. Unlike my siblings, I never complained about household chores and actively took the initiative to clean the house, do the yard, and set up for Christmas and other holidays.

I had aspirations and goals, which eventually led me to become a police explorer for the state police department and while being of service to the police department, I made sure my brothers got involved. My goal was to help them avoid the arduous journey to join the force and effortlessly pave a path for them. By that, I mean giving them a one-way ticket to a lifetime career, just like I had planned it all for myself.

I was 14 when I started and was consistently at the police station after school, assisting them with evidence, paperwork, and the jail itself. I was pushing myself hard to muck in and lend a hand whenever and wherever possible. Occasionally, I had the privilege of riding along with the officers.

My nightmares started when I was 15 years old while riding along with an officer. The memory is forever embedded in my mind. I clearly remember it was summertime and the afternoon heat was stifling. I was riding along on the swing shift, I rode on the day shift on the weekends primarily because I was in high school. The roster served me well. I was in a uniform. It was brown in color with explorer patches hemmed over it. I wore a black belt and black shoes. Apart from that, handy items in my possession were a flashlight holder and a key holder clamped tightly on my belt. If, while patrolling, the officers get a radio feed about a potentially dangerous situation, then the explorers are dropped off at a corner somewhere safe. But fortunately, they never felt the need to do that with me. I was an asset to them and excelled at everything most kids my age struggled with.

One day, we received a call. It was regarding suspicious activity. The area was in close proximity to where we already were. It was behind a corporate building, which was closed for the day. We were immediately dispatched to the location. The dispatchers informed us through radio contact that a suspicious-looking red VW Bug had been parked in the lot with the driver's door ajar.

When we arrived at the scene, the sun had set, the night fell, and the blue haze of the day had lifted to reveal the stars. It took us little to no time to reach the location.3 Upon arrival, we noticed that there was in fact a VW Bug in the parking lot with its driver's door wide open. Notable items that were strewn on the ground were a purse and a single red shoe next to the door. Suddenly, the air seemed heavy, and we immediately knew something was wrong. The officer looked at me and said, "You, go that way, and I will go this way." Nobody was inside the vehicle. The officer took the back of the building, and I took the parking lot and surrounding area.

I was walking around and noticed something; it was blocked by bushes. I stealthily walked over to that area and saw something just behind the bushes. They looked like look clothing. I warily inched closer and noticed a white female with her shirt pulled up over her head and her bra pulled down. She had blood pouring out of her mouth and her eyes were wide open looking slightly to the right as if she was frozen. I yelled for the officers, and he came running and ordered me to head back to the police unit and stay put.

He called for backup and in no time, there were several police cars. She was deceased. Her neck had been brutally snapped. I stayed out there until 2 am and my mother was furious at me because I had school. However, after she was told what I had stumbled upon her anger faded away and turned into concern.

To this day, the image of that woman gives me nightmares. The last gruesome piece of information I heard about the case was that the possible suspect was a dark color male who was seen getting on a bus down the street. After carefully examining the evidence, the officers concluded that she was taken from the fashion mall before her death. This was the beginning of my career in law enforcement.

The department I worked as an explorer for had assigned me to this one officer I used to ride with back in the day. I thought I knew the man well. To my dismay, I was completely wrong about him. Apparently, he met a woman on a domestic call and had raped her, after which he shot her in the head. I was there when they brought him into the station. My mind could not comprehend what I was witnessing; this was a man I trusted. His gruesome act still makes me shudder. I'm just glad he was convicted of the crime.

Chapter 2
Violence Reigns

At the tender age of 18, I had reached a higher level and was now a police cadet for a new department. The best part about this new venture was that I was provided with a uniform, and on top of that, it was a paid job. My uniform clearly had the word cadet imprinted on it, and it was right below the police patch on my shirt. Being a police cadet helps you prepare for the academy, learning the job without doing dangerous things. I was so excited to be in uniform with the police patches; I felt it was the next step toward my future. Also, I got to meet the Chief of Police and all the officers and listen to their jokes.

Before I get into my role as a young police cadet, I would like to take this opportunity to clear up a common misconception the general public has about the police. I'd like to start by addressing the word misconception; it's a wrong idea, a piece of misleading, incorrect information. It's false information covertly spread to influence public opinion or rather obscures the truth. With that said, I want to preface what I'm about to share is a truth most people are unaware of. The common misconception associated with police officers is that we are racists and blatantly act on that racism. This is far from the truth. Let's take the LAPD, for example. They hire to reflect the diverse community. You will find a huge percentage of black police officers and Hispanic police offers working for the LAPD. If there were even an ounce of racism or support for racism there, that most likely would not be the case.

What most people are unaware of is the fact that when we get in the car, we make sure we have all the necessary equipment with us. We log onto our computer, hit the clear button, and get on the radio and say clear. Whatever unit we are working for, it's the same procedure. Next, dispatch either sends you lower priority cases over the automated system or code two and higher cases like important calls, life or death kind of situations. The dispatch broadcasts it over the radio. So, in a nutshell, nothing is based on race of the caller. It's the automated system, the computer, that's telling police officers where to go. Yes, often when we do get there, we are dealing with a person of color. But remember, the radio calls directed the police officers to get to a certain location. We are not sitting in the car thinking, "Let me see if I can find a person of color to harass." We go where the computer tells us to go, where the radio tells us to go.

It's true that we don't live in a perfect world. There's good and bad everywhere, but the percentage of bad is small. People don't realize that at the end of the day, police officers want to make it home to their families safe and sound, having no regrets about doing something inappropriate. Racism is a terrifying picture the media has painted about police officers. And the media can have a powerful impact on an individual's thoughts and perceptions. We don't care what color you are. We care about your safety and the safety of the general public. We want to make sure our partner gets home safely, and similarly, our partners make sure that we get home to our families safely. Although, yes, there have been times when officers make mistakes, decisions must be made in a split-second because our lives are at risk. We only act when we see a threat. Nothing we do is based on the color of someone's skin. The media specifically takes shootings, and they throw things at you exaggerating how a white officer shot a black youth. They will put up his little league picture while stating how great he was. I'm not saying all shootings can be justified. All I'm saying is that police officers step out every day and react to the situation at hand when they are in certain locations that they were sent to by a radio call. It doesn't matter if you are black or white or Hispanic or an Italian when they get there. Police officers are not reacting to their color or their ethnicity but to the situation they are in. The priority of a police officer is the safety of all civilians. And that's exactly what my motive was. Safety.

Now back to when I was a cadet. It was a time of major transformation. By this time, not only was I on payroll, but I was also directed to carry handcuffs, and I always had a key holder on me. At the time, I was assigned to the police unit maintenance on the vehicle. There were several other, more intriguing, assignments like a jailer, evidence, and tech. I did dive into all of that at one point. We got to ride with officers and assisted them to the best of our capabilities. The city I lived in was well-known for gang activity, and the crime rate was significantly high.

While working for the maintenance unit, part of my duty was to drive the police car from the maintenance shop to the station. I clearly remember it was a clear sunny day around noon. We were given place cards for the windows that indicated a particular car was out of service. It was a safety measure.

Moving along, I remember driving on the main street, downtown. I was at an intersection when I stopped at a red light. I noticed a plethora of liquor stores and other shops across the street. Listlessly looking around, I was waiting for the light to turn green. What happened next is embedded in my memory to this day. Two armed robbers were in one of the liquor stores. One of them was armed with an AK47 while the other carried a 9mm. I watched them exiting the store. I looked across the street and noticed they had a vehicle on standby with a driver inside. As soon as the subjects exited the store, to their surprise, the first thing they saw was a prominent black and white police car. You'd think those notices displayed on the window of the car would stop them, but no. As soon as they laid their eyes on me, as soon as they saw the car, their immediate reaction was to start shooting, and that's exactly what they did; it was an intense moment. I am certain they could see a young kid with eyes wide open, terrified. I was scared to death, my heart pounding out of my chest. I had no weapon to defend myself. They kept shooting at me. Luckily, their aim wasn't exactly perfect, and the bullets bounced off the front of the road under the police car I was in.

In a state of fight or flight, I punched the gas and speedily drove straight off. I was yelling on the radio, "I need help," something that I think I should clarify is that when you're only a kid, all radio codes go out the door when you are in a horror-stricken situation, the kind that I was in. The bullets had hit the engine. Being seated inside a car saved my life. Unfortunately, the subjects got away at the time, but were soon apprehended. I remember my supervisor telling me how lucky I was.

I had another incident working with another officer in the field. This officer's arms were massive. He was about 6'2", and he was a bodybuilder. One day, we received a call to investigate a sexual assault and contact the mother of an eight-year-old boy. The boy was the victim and the uncle was the person of interest. After we received the information from the mother, we called for the Detective to respond. The detective was tied up in court, so we handled the investigation. The young boy was sodomized and was at the hospital for treatment and evidence collection. Being a police officer, you run into these cases almost every other week.

After receiving a statement from the mother and the boy, we went over to the person of interest's house, where he lives by himself. We could not find anyone else in any part of the house. The house was older and still had old fixtures and furniture. The subject was in his fifties.

When we headed to the subject's house, we contacted him at the front door. At first, we thought he would hesitate but to our surprise, he told us to come in. When we got inside the house, our eyes focused on the subject. We noted every move, every statement of his. While in the house, the subject was acting strange and weird. We observed how he had been drinking. We sat at a small dining table. I was behind the officer, and the officer was sitting across for the discussion. The officer started asking him questions. He started off by asking him, "Why do you think we are here?" and he said he could guess. The officer read him his rights, and he agreed to talk to the officer. The officer asked him to tell us what he did to the young boy, and he narrated the whole story with a big smile on his face in return. I noticed the officer started to shake a little, not liking what he had heard. Then the subject asked the office to try it as well with a very stern face. I was aware that this officer had kids of his own, too - and when the subject leaned over the table looking at the officer, he came unglued.

There was no way I could hold back or even stop this officer. The officer grabbed the subject and pulled him over the table. The subject was not winning at all. In an instant, I thought of calling the others. I got on the radio and called for help, and the sergeant was already pulling upfront to help with the investigations. I opened the front door and yelled to the sergeant that the situation had gone terribly and out of hand. The sergeant was not a small person either and very strong too.

The sergeant entered the kitchen and found blood scattered everywhere, and it was not the officer's. The officer was still on top of him, beating him, smashing his face. The sergeant could not get the officer off him, and he removed his rattail sap. The officers could carry them back then but were outlawed in the future. With one swipe, it knocked the officer off him, but he needed medical treatment because the side of his head was injured. The subject was transported to the hospital and was in a coma for quite some time, and the officer got stitches and was even sent for psychological evaluation.

Chapter 3
Face Off

I was on a ride-along with an officer as a cadet. We thought of resting at a place for a while. We were sitting next to a park close to downtown. When we sat down, the officer was finishing his report for the day when we suddenly caught the eye of several gang members sitting on a park bench. Their attire was kind of making it obvious for us to spot them as a part of a gang. The members were wearing blue bandanas and baggy pants. What caught my eye was a vehicle that kept driving by the park really slow and did not pay much attention to us police officers being around.

I informed the officer I was with. We discussed how to go about it and watched them pull into the parking lot next to the park benches. The other gang members were throwing signs with their hands toward the car. The car halted, and one passenger exited from the car's door wearing a trench coat. The officer and I noticed something unusual. We saw that the subject might have had something under his coat.

The subject then approached the gang members and showed his attention to one of them sitting down. Before we could say anything or move a bit more, to our surprise, the subject pulled out a sawed-off shotgun and, at point-blank range, shot another subject in the face, blowing half of his face off.

The other subjects, who were the gang members in the car, ran, and the subject with the shotgun just placed the shotgun down on the bench and sat on it, waiting for us to come and take him into custody. We called out the other units and took the subject into custody at once. He did not utter a single word all the way to the station. Later on, we found out that he was only sixteen years old and did this act for his homeboys. He probably wanted just to show off how cool and strong he was, whereas he was just in great trouble.

People, especially youngsters, don't really realize the impact such foolish acts can have on their lives or careers and all those who are related to them. Their name becomes black-listed. They have to go through several trial phases to be able to get out of such serious incidents. The younger the person is, the more they suffer. You can make the most of a long life ahead of you, whereas indulging in such scenarios just worsens the whole life. Being a part of the police industry, I see this sort of incident happen very often and mainly at a young age, which causes even more severe nightmares for the victim and the immediate family and friends.

At the young age of nineteen, I worked at a big mall as a part-time security officer. I would perform my duty there dressed in a uniform. It was a good job. I was satisfied with the duty I was assigned. Some other officers and I who were put on duty there on the same premises spent most of the time chasing thieves who would try to rob stores of things. Often, some people would tease other people coming to the mall or customers fighting with store owners over increased prices of goods. I would always end up breaking up fights. We carried our guns and batons, along with handcuffs and other equipment, as it was needed most of the time.

While working at the big mall, I was helping on the graveyard shift and was most of the time tired as it consumed most of my energy. My health was affected to a point where I came down with Viral Meningitis. I would suffer from fatigue and vomiting. I could not hold it in for long, so I went to two different hospitals to see the root cause behind my sickness. After taking second opinions from different doctors, I finally found out what was Viral Meningitis but had no way to treat it. Doctors at the hospital sent me to a bigger hospital in a more developed city for treatment. My sufferings were increasing. The pain was so bad and was becoming unbearable with each passing day. I had to do something about it as I had no plans of losing my job as the mall's security officer. I could not look into any light.

The hospital kept me in a room where there were no windows at all. It lacked ventilation, and it made me even more sick and stuffy. I noticed how only fully-suited people could enter the room I was kept in.

In the big room next to where I was kept, I could hear people screaming all night. I got very disturbed by all the noises. I would also feel concerned about it. When I asked people to see me about the room and the noises that followed, they told me that the patients kept there were suffering from severe spinal Meningitis. They further explained to me how some of those patients were incurable and might never be able to go out in public! It made me feel horrible for them, but it just made me want to fight the illness more. I wanted to get better. I wanted to get back on my feet and out of the hospital. Finally, I successfully fought the virus and was released from the hospital. Even though I managed to get out of that uncomfortable and displeasing environment, I was told that I would have to go through migraines and headaches for the rest of my life.

Chapter 4
Learning Where You Stand

I started working at the police academy. My excitement and eagerness to learn were at their peak. I went through pre-service solely on my own. I was very confident throughout that time. I knew I would be picked up while going through the academy. Some days were very exhausting and tiring. I would end up driving more than 50 miles a day to the academy, sometimes because of the heavy traffic.

I had become an early riser. I would get up at 4:00 am to get all my things ready. I would align my uniform, my badges, and what I would have for breakfast, etc. I would get home around 7:00 pm at night, tired and worn out after a long, tough day performing my duties. I was in perfect shape for the police academy. It made me feel thrilled and accomplished how I was mentally at the place and physically fit. My family was very supportive of my work and would motivate me to keep at it, especially my brothers. They would often tell me and remind me what to watch for a while I was at the academy. Being at the academy was not just tiring, but also quite stressful. It was a full-time job. Few could take being at the top the entire time. I would watch other recruits not make it for more than a week. Most of them could not keep themselves in shape and could not take much stress. There were about twenty-five different agencies and several pre-service recruits at the academy. While I was there, you could tell that some agencies that sent their new officers to the academy spent lots of money. Hence, the staff and administration at the academy treated them differently and really well. We started with 144 and ended with 42.

While at the academy, I was number one in the physical testing, whereas an agency recruit came second. I was doing 36 pull-ups and, at that time, broke the record of many other officers. I was good at the range and academics, but there were better recruits than me in that field! They made me the academy captain and gave me captain bars, but it put more pressure on me to get there earlier and take all the responsibility of the supervisors and recruits. While performing as a captain, I found out that a person put in as our president for the class was telling the tact staff all the things we were doing wrong. The president was voted in by the recruits to help us set up graduation and the awards ceremony. When I found out about this, I replaced him. The tact staff found out, so they ripped the bars off my collar and demoted me to being just a recruit. It was the last PT test they were given before the end of the academy. I noticed they called me out of the class and made me run for two miles in my hard shoes and uniform. When I got back, they called me for the test. They knew how tired I was. Despite that, I aced the test again. The tact staff made us shave our heads and burn our new academy hats in the last week.

Knowing my highest score, I was for sure to get an academy trophy, first place. When we had the big graduation ceremony with all our family members, they presented the awards and diplomas. My dad was sitting in the audience, accompanied by my mother. They announced the winner of the test to an officer for a department that was well known. I was amazed to see my dad stand up because he knew the scores and yelled, "This is bullshit!" What a shocker, but I moved on and got hired by a police department.

Chapter 5

The Dating Games

After I graduated, I started working for a Police Department and looked forward to a promising new career. I wanted to be one of the best officers and help people in need. Unfortunately, the city was right in the middle of two other big cities. It had a big mall and lots of traffic on the main street. I was on probation and was assigned to a field training officer. Field training officers are sometimes seasonal officers who have been around the department for a very long time. I remember the first day I started with an orientation, learning the stations, forms, and city. I was delighted when I was in my uniform and felt proud of myself for making my career.

Let me tell you something about my field training officer. He was married, he had no kids, and smoked and drank alcohol all the time. But he was good at writing reports and driving, which were some of the good points. While training with him, he spent most of his time meeting up with his girlfriend in the city and another fellow officer, who also had a girlfriend. I spent hours not training, sitting in the patrol car waiting to finish whatever he was doing. It got to where he was meeting this girl during every shift. These girls were not the angel type and could not hold a job most of the time. I noticed many times that when he was with this girl, he would tell the dispatch that he was not in the call area, and they would dispatch other officers.

I was not getting trained, and the Lieutenant was always asking for my evaluations, which were not being done under my field training officer. Everyone knew it was dangerous to report your field training officer or ask for a transfer to another one. I remember there was a robbery call, and on the way, I saw the suspects in a vehicle leaving the area, so I told my training officer. He said, "Let them go and we will make the report." I knew this was not for me. As the months went by in my training, the sergeant asked me for more tickets, which I could not provide him. I was agitated because of all this. I went home mentally affected by this, unable to change anything for myself. When the Lieutenant called me in and told me he was extending my probation, I broke down in front of him, and that is when I got transferred to another fantastic department that accepted me with open arms. My brother worked for the same department and was a detective, but he always did his own thing and was good at knowing all the criminals. My other brother worked for the Sheriff's department.

Chapter 6
What a Ride

My training for the new department went great, mostly because I had great trainers. I got off probation and was assigned to a graveyard. Most of our arrests were burglaries in progress: window smashes at businesses, gang shootings, DUIs, and fights at bars.

I was working the graveyard shift and came on at 10. Back then, we had an 8-hour shift, not like how it is today. I was assigned to the downtown area of the city in a police vehicle and was checking the business one by one when I came across a beat-up black van parked behind a steakhouse. The name of the steak house was Happy Steak. The steak house closed at 9:00 PM. I knew it was kind of late for deliveries, and I had never seen that van around before. I thought to myself that something was not right; I just had that feeling! I circled to the back of the van and noticed it pulling away. I was going to stop the van, but before I could make the move, a man came walking out of the back door.

He had a bandana on and a big tattoo on his neck. He was wearing an untucked shirt with khaki pants. At that time, I took my focus off the van and followed the subject walking on the sidewalk. I asked him to stop, through my window, but he started to run. I called for backup in the direction he was running. I noticed he turned down an alley into a bank's parking lot, at which he pulled out a chrome-plated .357 magnum revolver from his waistband, which looked huge, and he pointed at me while he was running. I shined my spotlight into his face, and it blinded him for a second, and then he started running again.

We ended up in a church's parking lot. He ran between two buildings, and I followed him with my vehicle and came around the corner. There he was in a combat stance waiting for me. He fired one round, hitting my lower driver door window frame and into my headrest, just missing my head. I could feel something on my left ear, but it did not stop me at that point. I exited the patrol vehicle thinking of my training, but also my wife and daughter. Is this worth it? I told myself it's my job and continued on foot chasing the subject. The subject ran down the sidewalk, and I had a clear shot, but a vehicle was coming in my direct line of fire, so I was unable to fire my weapon at him. At that point, he turned around, and I dove behind a wooden fence. He fired, hitting the fence, and I remember wooden pieces flying by me.

A .357 mag is a huge handgun, and depending on what round you put in it, it can get even more dangerous. I came from behind the fence and ran to the front of the church and noticed the subject crossing the street toward the park. I also noticed he fired a Hail Mary shot over his shoulder and it ricocheted above my head from a marble rustication on the church. I held my gun up and said, "Oh, God, hit him!" I fired three shots. The third shot hit him at fifty yards in the dark and flipped him over. The whole world responded after I had put out shots at the beginning. I ran over and noticed a blood trail in the park and thought to myself, no need for me to go into the bushes and wait for a backup. The backup arrived along with a K-9, and the search came up with the subject next to a house bleeding to death, sitting on his gun! Later, I found out I had shot the subject in his private part, and the bullet went out his left nut - ouch! The subject did rob Happy Steak, although I never caught the guy in the van. The subject was found to be a gang member and was one of Castro's soldiers. Years and years after his release, he shot and killed another person in a house and was arrested again for homicide.

Chapter 7
You Never Know

I was on patrol in my uniform when I received a call from a subject under the influence of a controlled substance (PCP). The report was that he was assaulting people in the community homes area. The description of him was big, tall, wearing shorts, and high-top tennis shoes. The community homes were not a place you patrol through. If you receive a call, two units must go in. The community homes were surrounded by wrought iron fencing and had a security guard shack at one end. The security was replaced numerous times because of the violence that had happened to them. It was not unusual for rocks and bottles to be thrown at us and our vehicles destroyed or lit on fire.

One of my friends on shift came to assist me. He was a tough officer, and no one could beat him one on one —he had fists of steel. We were both on the SWAT team. He was a corporal. Two stripers and the department believed in that program. His name is Steve Cabral. When the sergeant was not there, the corporal was the watch commander. We met outside the community, and he got into my vehicle, and we entered the gates. We noticed a lot of people drinking. I even noticed a person pointing over to the grass area between the apartments.

We parked our police car and went in on foot. We noticed the suspect we were looking for staring at us at a distance of about thirty yards. Before we could approach further, he charged at me like a bull. For some reason, he was focusing on me only. Before he could reach me, my partner's struck him to the ground, and he resisted. We finally got him handcuffed and noticed other people trying to tip over our police car, so we rushed the suspect back to the car, yelling at people to get back. We placed him in the back of the patrol car and started to get rocks and bottles.

My partner and I got back in and started driving toward the exit by the guard shack when we heard the subject in the back say, "Die, mother fucker, die!" The subject had a 22 automatic in his high-top tennis shoe, size 16. He fired one round at the back of my head and the bullet ricocheted off the bulletproof glass and went up and hit the light bar.

I opened my door, and my partner pushed me first. I will never forget that he did that. After we both exited the police car, the suspect rolled past the guard shack across the street and ran into a 7/11 store. No one was injured. A supervisor was watching this unfold and ran to the vehicle glass everywhere and removed the suspect from the back seat, grabbing the gun out of his hands while handcuffed.

Focusing on our police car and the rocks and bottles took our focus away from the suspect even though he had short pants, no shirt, and high tops - you never know!

Chapter 8
Glass Breaking

It was a cold weekend night with clear clouds covering the skies when I was coming back from the jail, dropping off an arrested individual with little to no traffic. The patrol cars were equipped with good seatbelts and had push bars in the front. The police cars were good to ride in or drive, and I never complained about our equipment because the Department always took good care of us.

I was driving down about 45 miles per hour on the main road in our city when I noticed headlights coming my way and paid no attention. The vehicle was traveling about 50 miles per hour. It was a large pickup truck. Before I could react or make any move, the truck came into my lane and struck me head-on. The impact was so great and intense that it broke the brackets on the seatbelts. I remember putting my arms up in front of my face and hitting the windshield. The damage to the front pushed the patrol hood and folded it like a piece of paper, and the hood ornament came right in my face. I remember looking out from one of my eyes. I saw the guys in the truck stumbling around the vehicles. Some citizens had stopped at the scene and had called 911 for help. The backup arrived accompanied by the fire department and the paramedic's team. They had to extract me from the vehicle. The driver was drunk driving and got arrested. He had several prior arrests.

The paramedics later told me that they could not believe their eyes at the damage to the vehicle and my injuries. They said I should have been dead as to how the accident had taken place. The paramedics also mentioned how someone was watching over me, which is why I was still alive and was breathing.

Later, I was transported to the hospital, where they examined me. I had cuts and bruises around my body, which just needed stitches. In addition, I had a concussion and took a couple of weeks off to get better and continue with my duties.

Chapter 9

De-Escalate

I was working on patrol on swing shift on a nice mid-afternoon when I observed a pickup truck with no license plates driving down the road. I was well known for letting people go on traffic violations because I hated writing tickets unless they were dangerous. I did not think they should be given tickets when a verbal warning might just be enough for them. I also had a good standing in the community and left it up to the traffic team to write tickets.

I pulled the truck over and noticed two occupants. The driver got out real fast when I exited the unit, and I told him to step on the sidewalk. A lot of time, you usually tell them to stay in the car. I noticed the passenger looking back at me, which reminded me of how it was a subject I was familiar with. I remembered he had felony warrants. I requested backup when the driver was trying to get my attention. I asked him if it was the person I thought it was, and he looked down and said, "Yes!" I noticed the passenger started moving over to the truck's driver's side, and I knew he would take off in the truck. I told the driver to stay where he was, and I went to the driver's side of my patrol car, and the truck took off. I entered my patrol car and started chasing the truck calling in pursuit who it was. I knew this subject really well. He was usually respectful to me, but drugs tore him down through the years.

I was aware he was heading toward the freeway and advised dispatch. When I entered the freeway, I noticed that the subject reached back and opened the sliding window from the cab. My heart started racing because I knew what was next. The subject produced a handgun through the window and started firing rounds at my patrol car. I radioed in that there were shots fired and continued after him, waving back and forth from side to side. The gun was a .380, so not much damage happened, but I was aware of how lucky some subjects get when they are shooting. After a while, I noticed the subject was out of bullets and threw the gun out of the window. I told all units that the subject had thrown the gun out of the window, and they needed to be at the location to recover it.

Now it seemed the whole world was involved. There were numerous police units and agencies at the scene. The sheriff's department was right in the middle, but I knew they did not care enough. He threw the gun out of the car right after he shot at the police, that's it. We did not know if he had any more guns or weapons in the truck.

My sergeant was behind me. The truck appeared to blow its engine and pull over to the side of the freeway, smoking heavily. We started a felony stop, and the sergeant was yelling "De-escalate" to the other agencies. The subject stepped out of the vehicle. He was so close to ending his life right there. The subject was then taken into custody, and the gun was recovered. When I walked up to the subject, he told me, "If I knew it was you, I wouldn't have shot, sorry!"

Chapter 10
Leaving the Tracks

I was working on patrol and was assigned a newly added duty. I was called an ID officer/CSI. I had the ID pins on my collar and was given a two percent pay increase. I was sent to a state university for additional training and attended a crime scene investigations course to get certified. From that point on, I would perform all crime scene investigations on my shift and if needed, I would be called out to crime scenes. I was given all the equipment for any crime scene and kept the equipment in the trunk of my patrol car.

It was a hot day while I was on my day shift, and I was working patrol when several officers received a call that a train had derailed at a certain intersection. Upon arrival, I noticed a gondola car had derailed at a crossing and hit a vehicle sitting at the down-arm section. The gondola car hit the car so hard that the engine was sitting away from the vehicle. The car was pushed into a concrete building. I was shocked to see it. I noticed an officer walking from the building. He was emotionally upset and told me that three girls were in that vehicle, and all had died. I did not know that the officer knew them. He was asked to leave the scene. I took photos of the scene and started walking down the track and located a wooden splinter. These are used to go under the wheels of the Gondola car. I looked around the area and saw two boys on bicycles looking at me. I noticed tennis shoe prints in the dirt where the gondola car was parked. I asked the boys to come to me, and when they did, one started crying and told me he had released the hydraulic brakes.

There were two sets of tracks at the scene, and when they released the brakes, the other train that went by on the other tracks set it in motion. The boy was taken into custody. He was too young to prosecute. Later that week, the railroad officials came to the station and told me I saved them a very large lawsuit.

The school was emotionally devastated, and the ironic thing was, that day, all three girls had given blood at the school to save other lives!

Chapter 11
Caring Person

I was on patrol in a graveyard and was coming back from the jail, driving on the freeway, when I noticed a tow truck sitting in the highway's center lane by itself. I passed it and saw it was a tow truck that we used in our city. I knew the driver because he always came to our scenes happy and tried to give us sodas. He was married and had kids. I was worried about him, so I pulled to the center lane and backed up.

I exited my patrol car and walked up to the tow truck. No one was in the truck's cap. I walked to the back and noticed the tow truck driver was lying upside down on his towing arm. The driver was hit by a hit-and-run driver and thrown into the truck. I felt his pulse and felt a very faint heartbeat. I called for the fire department/Paramedics. I noticed I lost his pulse and started CPR. I was giving him an oxygen supply, and, while doing so, he threw up. I had his blood and what I call eggshells in my mouth.

The truck driver did not make it. I went back to the station, and the sergeant was waiting for me. He saw I had blood on my uniform. He was aware of what had happened, and he also knew the tow truck driver. My shift was almost over, so he told me to go home and clean up. A few days later, they returned with his blood results, and he was negative for anything bad in his blood. Sad day!

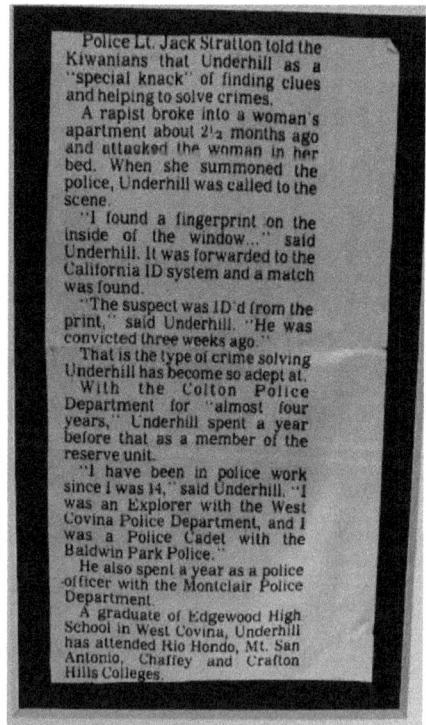

Police Lt. Jack Stratton told the Kiwanians that Underhill as a "special knack" of finding clues and helping to solve crimes.

A rapist broke into a woman's apartment about 2½ months ago and attacked the woman in her bed. When she summoned the police, Underhill was called to the scene.

"I found a fingerprint on the inside of the window..." said Underhill. It was forwarded to the California ID system and a match was found.

"The suspect was ID'd from the print," said Underhill. "He was convicted three weeks ago."

That is the type of crime solving Underhill has become so adept at.

With the Colton Police Department for "almost four years," Underhill spent a year before that as a member of the reserve unit.

"I have been in police work since I was 14," said Underhill. "I was an Explorer with the West Covina Police Department, and I was a Police Cadet with the Baldwin Park Police."

He also spent a year as a police officer with the Montclair Police Department.

A graduate of Edgewood High School in West Covina, Underhill has attended Rio Hondo, Mt. San Antonio, Chaffey and Crafton Hills Colleges.

Chapter 12
Victim

I was called to a crime scene in an apartment complex. It was a burglary or a rape case. The victim was found with duct tape wrapped around her head and hair, hands, and arms at the scene. The paramedics had to cut it off and remove her hair. It was so hard to witness all of that. The victim stayed silent and was talking under her breath. At first, she spoke to a female officer. She told the officer that the subject got in through the window and confronted her in the hallway. The subject held a knife to her throat and tied her up with duct tape. Then, he moved her to the bathroom, used the sink to get hot water, and poured it onto her private areas before he raped her.

I started investigating the scene by taking photos and gathering evidence and fingerprints. I was well known for getting ID hits on my prints, and I was really proud of this! I found the window from where the subject had entered and dusted it off for fingerprints. The subject removed the screen and rested it against the outside wall. I located a small print on the screen. It was a loop pattern and had some excellent points. When I put the fingerprint in the caller ID system, we instantly got a match. The match was of a male subject released on parole for rape several months before this incident. A warrant was issued, and the sheriffs picked him up and brought him to our station. The subject waived his rights. I told him I had gotten a print of his on the window screen, to which he said, "Damn, I had to take my sock off my hand to remove the screen. You're good!"

I remember how the defense was trying to say the print was on the outside and not on the inside at the court, but the judge had nothing to say about that except, "Come on, give me a break!" The next morning, the victim was there at the court to testify, and the news broke that she had taken her life! She was a university student and was an independent woman. Her mom and dad, along with her brother, were in another state when it happened. The subject pleaded guilty and was sent back to prison. The defense knew what had happened to her and would kill their case. I will never forget such cases, especially involving women being abducted or raped, or harassed. It is because of having a daughter and a wife around and witnessing such cases. I believe if it does not affect you in any way, something is not right!

Chapter 13
The Whole Family

I was working at a crime scene of a homicide when I entered a three-bedroom house, and the first thing I saw in the hallway was a twelve-year-old boy shot at the back of his head as he was running to get away. I then went into the first bedroom and saw a ten-year-old girl under the bed who had also gotten shot while trying to hide. I then went into the master bedroom, where the mother and father were shot to death lying on the bed. What drew my attention next was the bathroom floor, where a young girl was shot in the face. At the scene, I found out that a girl was lying on the bathroom floor. Her boyfriend was the main suspect, and I knew his name. So, I went outside to the front of the house and contacted the officer behind the crime scene tape. I asked them to keep an eye out for the subject when they advised me, he was standing there a minute ago and left on foot.

Later, we set up a wire at the cemetery on the gravesite with flowers where the victim was buried and was lying in a surveillance van. This went on for two days. We finally caught the boyfriend when he came to the grave, where he cried and said sorry countless times. We were setting up for a warrant and lost the subject. The next day we received a call that a relative had found out where the subject was staying and had knocked on the front door. When the subject answered the door, he shot him at point-blank range with a shotgun. And the case was over just like that!

Chapter 14
Ambush

I was reassigned to planning and training and was a corporal to two strippers. I received a four percent increase in my pay. I was also involved in hiring and training at the academy. I also oversaw the department stats and the motor officers. One of my main jobs was being a supervisor of the multiple enforcement department. The unit's responsibility was the high crime area and setting up surveillance on hotels and motels for parolees and crimes to businesses. We set up surveillance on the theater parking lot at night because of vehicle thefts and auto thefts. We set up surveillance in an insurance building as well, with tinted windows overlooking the parking lot. We took numerous subjects into custody and shut the thefts down.

I was driving around in a Ford LTD unmarked with a flip downright and siren. I overheard a grand theft auto had just occurred over the radio. While checking the area, I located the orange Corvette driving towards the freeway.

Two people had occupied the vehicle. I got behind the vehicle and called for additional units to assist. Unfortunately, the subject spotted me behind them and took off onto the freeway. I flipped down my light and noticed the Corvette was rushing over one hundred miles per hour. I was trying to keep up with them the best I could. Unfortunately, it was on a graveyard, and we had barely any other traffic. The Corvette then went on a cross-freeway that was even more secluded. Finally, the helicopter announced over my radio and said they were out of fuel and could not assist.

As I was following at a reasonable distance, I noticed dust had kicked up. I thought they had crashed and pulled up to the dust, but I noticed the Corvette was sideways on the freeway. As I exited my vehicle, I noticed the driver was still in the driver's seat. When I tried to pull my gun out, and even before I could bring it up ultimately, the second subject jumped up from behind the Corvette and started shooting rounds straight at me. It felt like tennis balls being shot at me. I was so shocked and petrified. I fired one round into the ground to bring my weapon up. I fired numerous rounds, but I knew I was way too high. The subject jumped back into the car and took off again. I had already called in shots fired and noticed my back tire had gotten flat. I was driving on the rim. The Corvette got off the next off-ramp when I stopped the pursuit.

The subject crashed into a dead end, and later, they were found hiding in a trailer. The parole tried to say that the kid driving was the one shooting at me, which was not true! They found one bullet hole in my vehicle and took the round out! I took a couple of days off and was then ready to return to my duty.

Chapter 15
Shoot or Don't Shoot:
Part A

I worked for the multiple enforcement team as a supervisor and was aware of the commercial burglaries occurring in the city's commercial area. So, I had my team and I covered that area in unmarked units. While paroling the area, I observed a subject coming out of the drive-through window at a closed Taco Bell. I approached the subject walking across an open parking lot and asked him to stop. I was about twenty feet from him when he turned around, holding a large hunting knife.

I asked him to drop the knife, but he did not listen to me and started walking towards me to hold the knife out. I asked him to stop, but he continued, so I backed off and told him to stop or else I would shoot him. After stepping back several times, the subject stopped and lay down the knife on the floor. I again asked him to throw the knife to the side and he complied. This subject admitted to doing all the commercial burglaries in the area and didn't care if I shot him to end his life.

Chapter 15
Part B

I was working on a patrol when I was called to a residential area regarding a man. He was walking down the street with a rifle, acting extremely confused. I came down the street when the weather was clear, and the sun was out.

I observed a subject walking down the street, holding what appeared to be a submachine gun. I positioned myself to the back of the subject as he was walking down the sidewalk. I pulled my weapon out and asked him to stop and not to point the gun at me. I warned him that if he turned toward me, I would shoot him instantly, so he needed to put the gun down that very moment. The subject took some time to think about it and finally placed the gun on the ground. I had him walk away from it, and when he did I quickly recovered it. The weapon was made of plastic. Thank God I was saved. It was yet another close call!

Man arrested: A Colton man was arrested for investigation of assaulting a police officer with a gun and transporting and possessing narcotics for sale after the car he was driving was stopped in Colton for a traffic violation, police said Monday.

Capt. Jack Stratton said $1,300 in cash and six ounces of methamphetamine with a street value of $6,000 were found in the vehicle.

Stratton said Vincent Miranda Ruiz Jr., 29, pointed a gun at Officer John Underhill as he approached Ruiz' car after it was stopped shortly after 9 p.m. Saturday for running a red light at Washington Street and the Interstate 215 onramp.

Underhill radioed for assistance and after other officers arrived, Ruiz was arrested without a struggle, Stratton said. A loaded .380 automatic pistol was taken from Ruiz, Stratton said.

Chapter 16
My Back and Hands Hurt

I was assigned to assist on a search warrant at a residence of a motorcycle gang. They needed people with metal detectors to search for a gun in a homicide. The information received was that the subject had buried it somewhere on the property. The Sheriff's Department got the warrant, and they asked for assistance from other agencies.

It was cold and very early in the morning. I noticed about a hundred people showed up and started looking when I walked around the house. The house was on a small ranch with a small fence in the back. It was about one acre outside the fence. I felt that the subject(s) may have buried it close to the gate at the back, so I started observing from there! I had been using a metal detector for years. I started with a cheaper one when I was a kid.

While roaming at the back of the house, I received a strong signal, and that is when I started digging. To my surprise, it was the handle of a bucket, so I pulled on it. It was attached to a big white bucket which was full of cocaine. I then found another bucket full of heroin, then one more, which had some more cocaine. I had found the gang's stash. It was getting late, and the other detectives wanted to leave. I told them I was not finished yet and continued looking around. I then hit something else and found the murder weapon wrapped in duct tape. The other detectives could not believe all that I saw and got out of the house. This case proved to me that one should always go by their gut feeling.

Chapter 17
A Close Call

I was working on patrol and spotted a vehicle at a high rate of speed and made a traffic stop on the freeway.

There was one occupant and a driver in the vehicle. I noticed the driver was moving around, but he could be getting his wallet or paperwork even. I approached the vehicle really quietly and just looked past the driver's door frame. It was dusked out and was getting dark. When I noticed that the driver had taken a gun out and pointed it at the window while waiting for me, he even rolled the window down for a good shot. I backed up slowly. We had those powerful spotlights on the sides of our cars and the takedown light on the light bar. The subject was blinded by the spotlight when I approached him.

When I called for a backup, the subject was armed. I then got behind the passenger door of my patrol car and just sat there, hoping the subject would not come out shooting.

Another unit arrived, and we did a felony stop which had the subject come out with his hands up. He was taken into custody without any incident. He had a gun, six ounces of methamphetamine, and $1,300 in cash in his vehicle, which we confiscated!

Chapter 18
Broken Back Questioned

I was working on the weekend as the Watch Commander on a day shift. I was the corporal, and the Sergeant was off that day. I was going through the reports and correcting reports at the station when I felt this certain urge to put caffeine in my body. I was craving a good cup of coffee. I was in a marked patrol car when I stopped at an intersection waiting for the light. It was then that a vehicle pulled up next to me.

Colton officer injured halting runaway auto

By TOMMY LI
Sun Staff Writer

A Colton police officer was in good condition Saturday after using his car to block a runaway vehicle that was believed to have been stolen by two youths, officials said.

The officer, whose name was withheld for his protection, suffered possible neck, back and internal injuries and was taken to Loma Linda University Medical Center, said Colton police Officer Cecil Nottingham.

Only one of the two juveniles in the 1984 Oldsmobile Cutlass was caught after a 15-minute foot pursuit by officers Nottingham and Bill Philpott, Nottingham said.

A 17-year-old San Bernardino boy believed to have been the passenger was arrested on suspicion of auto theft and obstructing an officer, he said. The teen's name was withheld because of his age.

By late Saturday, investigators were still looking for the driver, who was last seen in an apartment complex west of Reche Canyon Road.

The incident started at 1:25 p.m. when the officer tried to pull over the car traveling north on Hunts Lane, north of Barton Road, Nottingham said.

He was making a traffic stop because the car was believed to be stolen, Nottingham said.

The two juveniles were then seen bailing out of the moving car, forcing the officer to drive in front to prevent a possible head-on collision with southbound traffic, he said. The Oldsmobile struck the passenger side of the police vehicle.

Officers later caught the 17-year-old on Reche Canyon Road, south of Barton Road, Nottingham said.

The boy was taken to county juvenile hall in San Bernardino.

Officers still were trying to determine late Saturday who owned the Oldsmobile.

The car had four people sitting in it. The driver was looking straight ahead but was not looking at me. I noticed even waving at him that he did not look at the passengers and me at the same time. I got behind the vehicle and checked the license plate, and the vehicle came up stolen. I proceeded behind the vehicle and asked for assistance. I turned on my lights and noticed the vehicle had taken off, so

I called out a pursuit. The vehicle proceeded at a high rate of speed, blowing through the glow of the lights in the intersection. They then turned onto a two-lane highway - this highway was on a hill, and their direction was downhill. I noticed the vehicle slowed down, and the passenger and driver bailed out of the car, rolling on the ground and letting the vehicle move. My attention was on the vehicle, although I told the units the subject bailed and the direction of travel. The vehicle was heading towards an intersection and on the corner, people were doing a car wash event.

Underhill receives Medal of Distinction for work

By ED OLIVER

(article text illegible)

Distinction
Colton Police Department Cpl. John Underhill (center) received a Medal of Distinction from Colton Mayor Frank Gonzalez (at right) as the Second from Chief Jack Stratton (on the left). (Photo by Ed Elphick)

The suspects were booked into county jail in Rancho Cucamonga.

Colton officer injured: Colton police Cpl. John Underhill was bruised and complained of muscle pains after his patrol car went out of control on a rain-slick road while chasing a speeder and hit a dirt embankment early Thursday.

Underhill was treated and released from Loma Linda University Medical Center after the 2:45 a.m. accident at Randall and Eucalyptus avenues.

Capt. Jack Stratton said Underhill was chasing a pickup truck west on Randall and lost control trying to follow the pickup off the road into a sand hill area. The pickup was found abandoned by San Bernardino police near the crash.

San Bernardino police learned the vehicle was stolen and was regis-

I got my vehicle up to fifty miles per hour as the other vehicle got up to 40, and I cut in front of it before it reached the intersection, pushing my vehicle over and into a wall. I was removed from the vehicle by the fire department in front of a crowd of people. Some of those people at the scene found out what I did because they ended up in the ER waiting room asking about my stats. I will never forget that as long as I live. The hospital called my wife and told her my back was broken, and that was not true. I had the Admin of the Police Department standing over me saying, "Well, you should get a medal for all the things you have done." We ended up catching only two subjects that were inside the vehicle.

Chapter 19
Gave Up the Hard Way

I was working on patrol when a SWAT call-out was made on a subject. He was armed and had a handgun and confronted a resident in her home. I was assigned to SWAT as an assistant team lead. For some odd reason, I was always one of the first ones to enter the door. So I suited up when we were going to make an entry. It was a two-story condominium, where we entered through the front door. We tried to attempt to make contact with the subject, but unfortunately, he did not respond.

We entered, and I was the first one as usual. We did not find anything alarming downstairs, so we left from there. We then headed upstairs. I had one officer with me holding the shield in the front. Us officers know really well how stairs are extremely dangerous.

We took the stairs and reached the top. There, we

noticed that the subject had placed a mattress up against the bathroom door. So, we started pushing the door towards the inside, trying to move the mattress, blocking our way from going in. When I saw the subject standing in front of the mirror, he held the gun to his head, trying to shoot himself. We were kind of stunned for a bit, seeing him trying to kill himself and end his life. We instantly yelled at him to put the gun down, but unfortunately, he pulled the trigger.

I remember how shocked I was to see it and what it said. A hell of a day it was!

Chapter 20
Dirt Wall Wins

I came back to work after having taken several days off and was working the swing shift. It was wet because of the rain but had stopped. I was driving in a commercial area and the main street when I observed something strange and alarming. A white Toyota pickup with big wheels and a 4-wheel drive was parked at a distance.

I was aware of the thefts of these vehicles, which were happening in the area and other cities, and started driving behind them. I noticed it had no number plates and started to make a traffic stop, but the vehicle took off. I was in pursuit. I called it out to other units around while I noticed the truck turning down a dead-end road continuing on a dirt road. The truck was going at a very high speed, but I continued. The Toyota pickup drove onto the dirt road. I was somewhat unable to stop the vehicle and slid into a dirt wall. The front of my unit pushed up, crushing the bumper into the wall. The car did not suffer the damage alone, but I did. My legs got caught in the radio console and dash.

The vehicle had disappeared when one of the sergeants arrived at the scene and tried pulling me from the unit. It was not really a good idea to do that. The fire department showed up at the scene and escorted me from there. They transported me to the hospital as I was in major pain. My legs were severely hurt, but that's it, nothing else! The team found the truck down the dirt road, precisely where it was stolen, but unfortunately, the subject was never found.

I remember I was in the lieutenant's office when he told me with a smile that he was glad they had found that stolen vehicle that I had chased. So, as an act of valor, bravery, and recognition, I received the Medal of Distinction from a great chief and captain at the City Hall right in front of all the other officers, the council, and citizens. My wife, my daughter, my mother, and even my father were there. It was such a memorable and proud moment for me in my police career. It was videotaped, and I got it transferred on a CD. It's actually great because now CDs are going out of date. So, it was an honor that the medal came with a pin which you can tack on your uniform whenever you want and flaunt it in front of the world. I loved being a part of this department. I counted days from being promoted to sergeant in the future, but something drastic happened and changed my path.

Chapter 21
Family is Everything

I was working as a detective and had moved to a new house with my wife and young daughter. One fine day, when my wife was home with our child in her arms, she heard something at the back, the sliding door to be specific. She went towards the door where she had heard the noise, wanting to investigate what was happening. Even she had a strong police and detective-like instinct because of being around someone like me.

It was a subject with a crowbar prying on the sliding door handle. My wife grabbed the phone instantly, still holding onto our child really tight and called 911. My wife showed the phone to the subject to let him know she was calling the police through the glass, but he did not care about that. The 911 dispatch called me, and I was on my way to code three red lights and a siren. I was only five minutes away from my house while the dispatch stayed on the phone with her, keeping a close ear on what was happening and not losing any contact with her. Unfortunately, my wife lost sight of the subject. I arrived at the scene, but the subject had already gone. My wife asked to move to a safer place for our betterment. She was worried about our child growing up in that area. She strongly felt the need to shift from there as she did not feel safe or secure, so I agreed. It was a tough decision because it took me a lot of time to settle in at my workplace, but I firmly believe that your family comes first before anything else.

I found a very beautiful place to move to that had an ocean view. It was surrounded by fresh air, and most importantly, it was right by the beach as I kept in mind how much my wife admired and loved the beach—a very safe place. So, I got myself transferred to that area's police department. I did not want my work to suffer as well because of relocating. So, I was happy to be appointed to work at the nearby graveyard there. I was also given a map for me to look around and find places. The most beautiful thing about being appointed at that location was that you could park your police car next to the stunning cliffs and just sit there, observe the ocean, how the waves were buzzing and crashing with its dormant strength, gently drenching the golden sand with ice-cold water. It made me feel free, surreal, and honest, at that very moment. Even though we managed to settle in really well at the new place, we were unaware of whether the community would accept us, especially my child and my wife. Our child was having a hard time at school. He was unable to focus correctly.

The sudden shifting really did affect him. He was not able to adjust to the new environment that easily. The mothers from school had a group that would socialize in their group parties and had become excellent friends in a short while. But unfortunately, they did not include my wife or even me in their group, for God knows why.

My brother was a sheriff, and he worked with one of the sergeants at the department where I had gotten transferred. My brother worked with the sergeant closely before he was transferred from another agency. My brother told me to be careful of him. He spent a long time experiencing the sergeant's kind of person and gave me a heads up for staying vigilant around him. For example, my brother told me how the sergeant was known for stabbing people in the back. This was quite disturbing for me at first, but I assured my brother that I would be careful and away from danger. The sergeant seemed like a nice guy to me, so I did not really push myself to move away from him.

When it comes to law enforcement agencies like mine, there is a lot of ego. Every individual in the department takes their self-respect and worth very seriously. All the things that I did and all the actions that I took in the past helped me get hired at the police department, but it almost felt like starting over, even though I had a lot of experience. Some supervisors at my department did not like that and felt intimidated by it.

Chapter 22
The Phone Booth

I was working the swing shift when it stopped raining in the afternoon. I received a radio call about a man in a phone booth threatening suicide. I was the first unit there and noticed the subject was armed and yelling out of the phone booth: "My life is over." So, I positioned myself in a safe location and started talking to him while I advised the other situation unit. The subject was a young man. He was very upset about his life and how people treated him. I talked to the subject for approximately thirty minutes.

I tried to comfort him to not attempt suicide. I told him I would be his friend if he didn't harm himself or anyone else. After several minutes had passed, I had successfully told the subject to lay the gun down and walk to me. I had placed him on a 72 hold, and after he got out, I immediately contacted his family and had them meet him. I knew his family would be better at stopping him from doing so and helped him get out of it. Later, I wanted to check up on him, so I spoke to him on the phone several times and noticed that he was talking about getting a job. His family told me that he was doing great now. The sergeant appreciated me saying: "Great job!" I even received a commendation from the Chief. I went along with the Chief, and he told me "I guess this is not your first one" as he had rewarded me once before as well and that he remembered. It felt great.

Chapter 23
Back In Detectives

The Chief and Commander opened a new position for a narcotic investigator, which was the very first one to be initiated in the department. I got that position first and started right away. I was sent to the Narcotics Investigation School and also the search warrant school. I had already had some experience from before, which had helped me get the position. The Chief pulled out of the narcotics task force, which did not make them happy because of the funds, but I had to work with that. I did not cause any issues.

I worked for a Detective Sergeant, the one my brother had warned me about earlier, who was a bit difficult to work with, but it was going fine. He let me work the case without micromanaging me. He gave me a lot of space to make amends my way. In a month, I performed around thirty search warrants and collected large amounts of cases regarding drugs and money.

Chapter 24
He is All Dried Up

I was working really hard on a case of a known heroin dealer. I asked the task force if it was okay for me to work with this guy, and they told me "He is all dried up" and gave me the go-ahead. I set up surveillance for two weeks and watched him make deals. Finally, I got a search warrant and found hidden in his 2x4s that he built the shelves of one of the highest heroin seizures in the county.

Chapter 25
Close Call on Wire

I was working undercover on a case which involved 500 pounds of marijuana in a U-Haul. I had to be wired up and show up at the main subject's house to make the deal. This guy had a family, which included his kids and a wife. He lived in a lovely house and had luxurious cars parked outside his house. I had no idea what I was walking into. I felt a little skeptical at first. Another detective and the sergeant monitored the wire transmission, while I went inside the house.

I walked up to the front door and heard someone come in. I entered, and the main subject was pointing a .45 Cal auto-straight at my chest. I started to get past the man and played the part saying: "How can we make a deal with one pointing that gun at me?" This time the sergeant and other detectives were freaking out and hoping I would not get shot! The subject told me while laughing, that if I were a cop, I wouldn't have said that and instead pulled my gun, so it's alright. He put his gun down, and we made the deal.

The drugs were successfully recovered after the deal. The subject lost everything and was convicted of transportation and sales. Our department told the DEA, and they were involved in the case as well after the seizure.

Fortunately, everything was going great for me, but the department was going through a lawsuit and investigation for some incident that occurred before I had even started there. So, some of the information had me worried.

Chapter 26

The Badge: A Simple Act of Trust and Honor

One day, I came to work early and was getting ready for court on a case. The evidence room was kept up by another detective who had a key. When I entered the evidence room, I knew the section that held the drugs I recovered and the money. When looking for my evidence for court, I noticed numerous envelopes open and dope and cash missing. The further I checked, the more I found available.

After seeing this, I knew I had to report it, so I went to my sergeant, who was a good friend of the detective in charge of the evidence room. This was the first mistake. The investigation should have opened at that time, but the sergeant and commander did not want to push the issue. I noticed this later. I saw their attitude changing, and how they were getting distant. I was well aware of who had taken the drugs and money from the evidence collection, and they knew it as well. I asked the sergeant how I was supposed to go to the court if the evidence that I had collected was missing, to which he told me that they might not even go to the court. This made me feel very uncomfortable and uneasy. I was unable to work under those conditions. I was someone who abided by all the rules and acted accordingly. I never had the intention of scoring more than anyone and would only do what I was asked to do. I was not used to bribery or anything that went against my morals of being a police officer. I did not like how officers were into stealing anything, and it went against my core values in the Law Enforcement department.

Chapter 27
The Time to Retire

I was working an undercover case in a hotel and was waiting for a kilo deal. I had the money and I was wired with a microphone. My backup team and sergeant were standing by as I thought. I looked out of the window and saw two subjects approaching me. They both were heavily armed. It was a setup to shoot me and take the money I had recovered. I called the sergeant and asked for help. The sergeant told me it would take them time to reach as they were at the station. They were supposed to be outside setting up to provide backup but weirdly they were not there. I was all alone there waiting to get attacked by those armed men. I was trying too hard to escape somehow. I had gotten so confused.

I was able to get out of the bathroom window before they kicked the door to open it. I ran out of the hotel and rushed straight to the back of a restaurant. Luckily, the men had left. It was at that very moment when I thought to myself that it was time for me to retire. What a ride I had that day. My wife was so happy and felt proud of all the actions I took and how I performed my duty with the utmost honesty and valor. She told me that if I had stayed in, we could not imagine what would have happened to me. I later on got to know that the detective who was stealing the evidence was caught a couple of years later and had gotten convicted. Several officers called me and told me about it and expressed their sorrow about the whole thing. They also mentioned how the staff felt sorry for the officer who stole the evidence.

Chapter 28
The PI World

After I retired, I still loved being part of investigations. I received my PI license and opened my business. The PI and this business were exciting but different. I could not be a part of all the cases I worked on as a PI because some were boring and did not interest me. I stayed away from defense work and focused on what I could do to help people and facilitate them however I could. It's hard for PIs to make any money unless you have solid contacts with other agencies or companies. I made all those contacts because I had retired.

I started working on missing person cases. I did have cases of this sort earlier in my career too when I was working as a detective with the police department. After working on numerous cases, I started giving classes to investigators and search groups. I shared my experiences with them and taught them how to go about certain cases. I thoroughly shared my expertise with all the detectives/volunteers so they could benefit from it, too.

After a while, I became well-known and renowned to by the search and missing groups online and started receiving almost twenty calls a week on missing person cases. I was unable to work on all those cases, so I advised on searching and investigations only. I worked many cases and, mostly, I did not get paid for them. It was a total of 7000 pro bono hours. The reason for this was that the families of the missing people did not have the resources to pay for a private investigator - as people know, most private investigators charge fifty to a hundred dollars for just an hour, plus the extra expenses included as well. I remember traveling thousands of miles and staying at houses, hotels, and sometimes even in my car. These cases made me exhausted, but it's what I wanted to do, you know. I wanted *more feathers for my wings.*

Chapter 29
Another case

Another case I had was a missing person case. A husband was missing, and no one knew where he was—a hard-working family man with young kids. The wife asked me to try to find him, and I promised myself to make it happen for the family. I traveled over 6000 miles searching for the man.

The wife was an airline flight attendant and would sometimes be dropped off by her husband. When her husband went missing, she went down to the big airport and contacted the police chief and the parking officials. They advised that if he was there, they would find him, but they never looked. His dead body sat in a parking lot for almost eight months behind the wheel of his work truck. The stain from his body fluids left a large circle around the car. Some citizens smelled something terrible and reported it. That's how they found him. I would have checked that same parking lot if the authorities had not said they would. I drove by that same lot off the freeway going home and checked all the outer roadway. The attorney handling the family's case was John Anthony Picerno, a person who cared about families and was always professional.

After years of being a PI, I retired from the field and believed people could succeed if they tried - that they could make a difference in everything they did! I was not a heavy-handed law enforcement officer; I believed in thinking before acting and responding right to the situation. One thing I always knew was that I could die wearing a badge, but it was my job! Like any other job, the good or the bad. So be safe and help others!

Chapter 30
The Pond

Being a private investigator through the years, I did take my beating from the Law Enforcement department. It did not matter to them what I had done before. They saw me like I was some threat. As we all know, Law Enforcement personnel have a huge ego. They hated me if I would point out any mistakes that they made or make their mistakes come to light. But it was okay with me. I remember how one day I was working on a missing case. The sheriffs searched for the subject while I drove out to the search area because the family wanted me to do so. You always need to keep in mind that you work for the family, and not for the Law Enforcement department. It's your job to look after the case with complete honesty and not look for your personal interests and gains.

When I arrived at the search area, I noticed a lot of searchers. They appeared to be from the Sheriff's academy. I asked the lieutenant whether I could be of some help, but he asked me to leave. I identified myself and told the lieutenant that the family had sent me there, but he paid no attention and again asked me to leave. I immediately walked away.

They searched over 600 acres of the area but found nothing. So, I returned the next day and searched by myself. I luckily located the subject in a pond. Do you think the sheriffs were happy that I had found the subject? Most certainly, no! The sheriffs knew the subject, but they did not like him so they didn't work thoroughly. The subject was known to use drugs.

I was asked by the subject's family to attend his funeral, so I went. I remember seeing the video on the wall and the pictures when he was a child, and it almost broke my heart. Officers only focus on their job and promotions and forget that the subject was not just a victim but he was someone's son first, and that is how they remember him.

I never looked at a person for who they were, and if they were missing it was my job to find them. Yes, in hundreds of cases, you find no one but hope is everything to these families. When working on these cases, the outcome is not good most of the time. You can't just say: "I will not get into his case. It hurts too much." After you find a runaway and return them home, it is not over for the parents. It is like the beginning, and when that runaway is gone for good, it is devastating, and you always tell yourself if only you could have done something more for the family.

www.ingramcontent.com/pod-product-compliance
Lightning Source LLC
Chambersburg PA
CBHW051544120626
46551CB00013B/1363